DRESSES FROM THE OLD COUNTRY

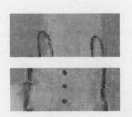

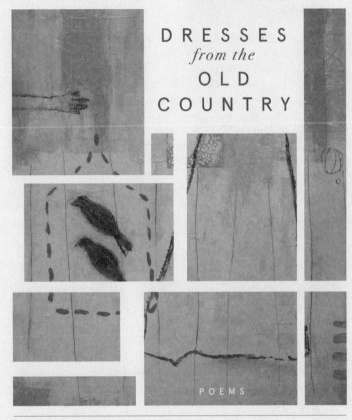

DRESSES
from the
OLD
COUNTRY

POEMS

LAURA READ

AMERICAN POETS CONTINUUM SERIES, NO. 168

BOA EDITIONS, LTD. ❧ ROCHESTER, NY ❧ 2018

First Edition
18 19 20 21 7 6 5 4 3 2 1

For information about permission to reuse any material from this book, please contact The Permissions Company at www.permissionscompany.com or e-mail permdude@gmail.com.

Publications by BOA Editions, Ltd.—a not-for-profit corporation under section 501 (c) (3) of the United States Internal Revenue Code—are made possible with funds from a variety of sources, including public funds from the Literature Program of the National Endowment for the Arts; the New York State Council on the Arts, a state agency; and the County of Monroe, NY. Private funding sources include the Lannan Foundation; the Max and Marian Farash Charitable Foundation; the Mary S. Mulligan Charitable Trust; the Rochester Area Community Foundation; the Ames-Amzalak Memorial Trust in memory of Henry Ames, Semon Amzalak, and Dan Amzalak; and contributions from many individuals nationwide. See Colophon on page 96 for special individual acknowledgments.

ART WORKS.
arts.gov

State of the Arts

NYSCA

Cover Design: Sandy Knight
Cover Art: Belinda Bryce
Interior Design and Composition: Richard Foerster
Manufacturing: McNaughton & Gunn
BOA Logo: Mirko

Library of Congress Cataloging-in-Publication Data

Names: Read, Laura, author.
Title: Dresses from the old country : poems / by Laura Read.
Description: First edition. | Rochester, NY : BOA Editions, Ltd., [2018] |
 Series: American poets continuum series ; no. 168
Identifiers: LCCN 2018015160 (print) | LCCN 2018018260 (ebook) | ISBN
 9781942683674 (ebook) | ISBN 9781942683667 (pbk. : alk. paper)
Classification: LCC PS3618.E224 (ebook) | LCC PS3618.E224 A6 2018 (print) |
 DDC 811/.6—dc23
LC record available at https://lccn.loc.gov/2018015160

BOA Editions, Ltd.
250 North Goodman Street, Suite 306
Rochester, NY 14607
www.boaeditions.org
A. Poulin, Jr., Founder (1938–1996)

CONTENTS

⮌

for Brad, Ben, and Matthew

There was a choice of pie for dessert, and one was blueberry and one was apple, and the waitresses were the same country girls, there having been no passage of time, only the illusion of it as in a dropped curtain—the waitresses were still fifteen; their hair had been washed, that was the only difference—they had been to the movies and seen the pretty girls with the clean hair.

—from "Once More to the Lake" by E. B. White

In Praise of Shadows

Junichirō Tanizaki says the Japanese
love shadows, their lights low
when they eat, their silverware tarnished.

Tanizaki asks, *Why so much shine?*

He wants to raise the lacquered bowl
to his lips and stare into its darkness,
a lake you can slip inside,

your body glowing like the moon
casting its own shadow on the surface,

larger, smudged, a moon
that's been crying, its face puffy and soft.

What kind of child names her yellow dog
Shadow? How did I know she would become
the shape of our grief, following

my mother's body when she went down
to do laundry, the sheets always needing
to be changed, at the end several times a day?

Last night I dreamed of a canvas
with something painted in each corner,

a girl, a boy, a window, water.
I could only see one piece of the painting

at a time, I was sick and fever burned
my sheets, but every time I woke up,

I knew I had to go back under.
Someone was down there

who had to be saved.

I

VACCINATION

The scar on my arm is thin like the skin
of a fruit close to splitting.

It marks my birth as before '72,
before the end of smallpox but after polio,

after the wheelchairs and the iron lungs,
the radios crackling with war.

If you were born then, you remember
taking your Halloween candy

to the fire station to have it checked
for razor blades. Maybe there was one

black girl in your class like Martha Washington
who brought upside-down clown cones

for her birthday and then moved away.
You watched the *Challenger* blow up

on the news again and again.
I was there in my boots and eyeliner,

waiting by the wall until a boy
asked me to dance. His mouth was a shock

of salt. I flicked my name off like ash
from my cigarette. I loved how the tip

flamed, like the squares of coal
in our furnace. Maybe you remember

my father. He was thin and transparent
like the place where the needle went through.

Maybe I can peel it off, the dead skin
from a burn, the kind we got back then,

before sunscreen, when we just took off
our clothes and got in.

HERE IS A MAP

Tinker lived across the street
next to the house we walked by fast
because someone was shot there.

That dog barked all night at Shadow.
In the summers, we had her hair cut
close to her skin and they put bows

on her ears and sometimes Tinker
got loose and came running over.
He was so thin he could slip through

the gap in the fence and we had to put
Shadow in the house. This is where
we first saw it, when we came home

from church, Tinker on Shadow
and Shadow crying, the ribbons
on her ears undone, my mother yelling,

Get inside. The boys across the street
saw it too: Tim, who brought
his ZZ Top record over just to play

"Legs" and watch my face
when they sang, *Shit, I got to have her.*
And Sean, his brother who never spoke,

who shot himself in that same house
behind the white paint and the hedges.

THE SUNSHINE FAMILY

My mother ordered a boy doll from New York
because she wanted us to understand
anatomy, so my brother held him
underwater until he was full
and then yanked him up to watch
the stream pour from his plastic penis.
I had a girl doll named Chrissy
with red hair and brown eyes like me.
I drew cuts on her arms with a Bic pen
then covered them with Band-Aids,
pulled her in the wagon to the hospital, her face
and body under a blanket
so all you could see was her hair.
I was scared when I went
with my friends to parties and all the boys
crowded around the keg and brought us
cups of beer, one after another and then
laid us down behind the bushes.
I couldn't remember their faces later
when I came home and knocked over
the vase of flowers I had given my mother
and laughed as I knelt in the puddle of dead
petals and tried to clean it up.
My brother saw in my eyes
the gravel pit in Cliff Park
and tried to hide me from our mother.
The Christmas our father died, she bought us
The Sunshine Family instead of Ken and Barbie,
the man with black hair and a sweater vest
clean and smart like our father,
the mother blond and small-breasted
in jeans and a bandanna
like our mother the Saturdays she came down

to our rooms to clean and we had to get out
of her way. She was angry at us
for not keeping things neat
the way she'd taught us.

ADRIAN*!*

Sometimes at dinner, we could get her
to do it. We had watched the *Rockys* together
and we all agreed *Rocky II* was the best,
there's the baby and Adrian's coma
and Rocky sitting in the chapel and Adrian
finally waking up and telling him to *Win.*
And that last scene after the fight is over
when he's looking for her in the crowd
and he sees her and yells *Adrian!*
and you can hear in his voice how he almost
lost her. This is what we want from my mother,
an unlikely Rocky, 5'1", blond, and Irish,
but she can do a perfect *Adrian!,* Rocky pouring
out of her and shocking all of us into laughter,
this woman who lost one husband
and was now sitting next to another,
who irons all her clothes on Sunday nights
and polishes her shoes like her father taught her,
who goes whole workdays without stopping
to go to the bathroom or eat her yogurt,
was suddenly an Italian boxer, sweating
and crying. When we asked her, she always
resisted a little at first, I think she felt
she shouldn't want to do it, but we had
to hear it, that yell deep inside her,
a body dragged from the river.

FLASHDANCE

The year I was thirteen, I worked in a steel mill by day
and as an exotic dancer at night like all my friends

in eighth grade. We were tired but about to get
our big break. Since we were all Jennifer Beals,

we wore leg warmers to keep our calves loose
so we'd be always ready to show what we had.

We cut the necks out of our sweatshirts so they slid
off our shoulders even though our mothers

made us wear shirts underneath. I didn't tell
the other Jennifers how I went down to my room

in the basement where I moved after my mother
remarried and started to have new children

and played "Maniac" and tried to run in place
as fast as the real Jennifer, so fast you couldn't see

the magic. Like those cartoon flip books,
each drawing only different by one small move.

And then came the song when she shows everyone
what's under her welder's mask and overalls,

a body that can fly across a wood floor and land
in a somersault. I had to pretend the flying part—

there wasn't enough room between my bed
and the accordion door my new father installed.

I lived in a warehouse like Jennifer.
I couldn't believe it when she went to dinner

at the seafood restaurant with that man and slid
her foot into his lap. I thought it must have felt

like the lobster she was eating,
something I'd never had.

BALI HA'I

Bali Ha'i, my mother sings to me
in the kitchen, one hand on my waist,
the other turning me in circles.
I've never seen *South Pacific,* but I know
it's about an island where the sun
is too hot to cry, where the girls wear
skirts made of long grass like that doll
who dances on the dashboards of cars
old men drive. This linoleum is a pattern
of brown squares, the earth from a plane.
I am fourteen and embarrassed
because I cry every day after school
and this is all she can think to do.
After *The Carol Burnett Show*
and the peanut butter crackers,
after Mark who said, *What the Hell*
when I asked him to the dance,
after algebra and mononucleosis
and my mother's fifth baby
and singing "I'm Just a Girl
Who Cain't Say No" when I tried
out for the play and didn't make it,
after my new father dragged his suitcase
of silence through every room.
This is not my kitchen. And I don't
know where Bali Ha'i is exactly
except somewhere in the South Pacific.
Or why I can't say no or what
I'm even being asked.

Renaissance Body

You were a man but they needed you to advise
the cheerleaders, which is how I came
to be lying face down on the floor of your classroom,

drawing bubble letters on a sign for a boy's locker,
telling him to *Go,* as if he wouldn't have without me.
You leaned over me, and Barbie, who was actually

named Barbie but was so nice you had to forgive her,
and showed us some paintings in a book of art
you were using in class and looked at Barbie,

and said she was beautiful like the women
in the paintings, who were naked.
And then you looked at me and said I had more

of a Renaissance body, and I thought it was too bad
I was smart because I knew exactly what you meant,
the plush, pink women in the paintings of Rubens

and Titian, their thighs thick as trees,
and shame came down over me like the shades
we had back then with the pull cords and the small

rings at the bottom which I sometimes
stared through when I couldn't sleep, wanting
the world in miniature.

I lived next door to your wife's parents,
your wife whom you left, who got a job selling bras
at Penney's and always asked after my mother.

The night her father fell on that porch, my father
jumped over the fence and pushed on his chest
again and again but there was no rescue,

only an ambulance and a man's body
being slid inside it, your children watching.
You had one perfect daughter, long hair that curled,

straight A's, her body slim and easy for the boys
to lift. But I liked your other daughter better,
the one who rode the bus all day

and talked to herself. She cut her own hair
and crocheted hats. We never spoke.
But we knew each other.

GHOST CLOTHES

Every day I drive past the dead
and listen for their sighing
the way you could hear
people talking in a diner
and spoons hitting coffee cups
in a song I used to love.
One of those stones is my father,
never getting old, never falling
asleep in his chair or leaving
fruit out on the counter.
He should take off his ghost
clothes so we can watch reruns
and talk about the weather.
And if a storm comes up,
we'll close the windows and sit
inside the dark house or maybe
go out into it. Like the day
I graduated from high school
and my brother and I ran
through the lightning and rain
to the playground where we swung
on the metal swings that always
kept swinging and creaking
when the bell rang and the kids
jumped off so I had to stay back
and hold onto the chains until
they stopped. My brother and I
stayed out too long, so I threw on
my cap and gown and ran into line
and some kids were high
and one girl was pregnant
and I had this storm inside.

Alaska

After he gets back, my brother keeps
talking about the light, how little there was
of it, he was pouring it in a pitcher,
cupping it over a basin. The last time
I was there, it was summer and we had
too much of it, it was all over us.
I was fourteen, visiting my friend
who had moved away. We rode our bikes
out to the glacier and stood beneath
its waterfall, we camped in the Yukon
where you could see the minerals
in the rocks, we lay on the ferry's deck
and watched the Northern Lights
tear open the sky. At the hot springs,
I went into the wrong bathroom,
but I didn't leave even when I saw
the bodies were the bodies of men,
red from the showers, their eyes staring
back at mine like the eyes of animals
caught between trees. My brother's still
cold, he won't take off his coat, he huddles
over his amber beer like it's a glass of fire.

THAT LAST TIME

First the babies came and my parents moved me
out of the room with the yellow roses
and the curtains that lifted in the breeze
and the statue of Mary in the McCulloughs' backyard
that glowed in my sleep
into the basement with its concrete floors
and the light switch you had to turn on and off
with a broom so you wouldn't feel the shock.
No window. A cork wall where I pinned
my dead corsages. In college, I took the room
converted from the garage. Thin walls like arms
around my ribs. Plastic on the windows,
wildflowers growing up tall in front of the house.
A separate door where a boy came and went.
Did I imagine him? That last time,
weeks after I thought he was gone for good?
He just came in and lay down.
His shirt was white and soft from washing.
I told myself I wouldn't fall asleep, but I did.

Introduction to Poetry

Professor Nordhaus assigned me
Galway Kinnell's "The Hen Flower," section 2
of *The Book of Nightmares*, instead of section 3,
"The Shoes of Wandering."
Who wouldn't rather go with Galway
to The Salvation Army to try on "these shoes strangers
have died from"? But instead, I got the hens,
unable to understand the ax or the eggs,
and me, not getting why it was the hen
who helped Galway know
how little he knew, how we sleep on the feathers
of hens, how these feathers are all that lie
between us and darkness.
How hard it must have been to write
"Listen, Kinnell," and then to stop writing and listen
to the hens in their sawdust beds.
How hard it was to read and then go back
to my room in Grace's house where she let me stay
for free while I went to school
so I could learn again and again that everything
dies, even the poem, even Galway
who died this week and brought me back
to that classroom where I sat behind
a dark-haired girl named Mona.
She only spoke once in class, the day we discussed
a poem called "Breasts." I learned then that she wasn't
shy, she just didn't care much for shoes
or hens, but breasts she liked, she kept almost
cupping her own under her sweater as she talked
about the poem until I thought she was going
to actually show them. Which is where I think
the poem was going.

THINKING OF YOU

My mother tells me she saw Greg and he asked
if I was married, and I think of how he used to run

down the hall of our high school to open the doors
for me into Senior Hall with its rows of blue

lockers, the smell of amphibians in jars, how
he sent me roses in a box with *Thinking of You*

printed on it, and he was, turning his flushed face
towards me like a lamp during Religion.

My mother tells me Greg lives alone now
on his family farm, growing wheat and alfalfa.

I can see him there, behind his gingham curtains,
and I think this is where youth is kept,

all these years since have been moving
like the creek at the edge of Greg's property

but the farm is the same, the grain turning gold
every night. This was the color of the future.

The color of the walls of the restaurant
where the boy I really loved works now,

I don't have the courage or I'd go there some time,
sit alone at a table with a silk rose and a candle,

order Chardonnay and watch the light catch
in the glass. Greg thought I was kind.

When someone loves you like that,
you should pay attention. You shouldn't drive

all night with Dave up into the mountains of Idaho
until Coeur d'Alene Lake is too far

below you, a black hole like the ones you read about
in school. You could float on that lake forever,

the sound of a motor telling you its story of speed,
how it can turn water over so you can see

its white underside, how you could get caught in it,
your body a red bloom in the water.

GLOVES

On the last night of class, he left
his gloves, gray wool, fingerless.
They smelled of smoke
and work, and I wondered where
he wore them and if his hands
were cold now on the steering wheel
of his truck as he drove off
out of the city.
He is young but already his hair
is thinning and the creases
around his eyes deepen like rings
in the center of one of the trees
he splits, his fingertips cold,
their whorls printing the ax.
I am young but starting to settle,
like floorboards and faucets.
Soon my husband and son
will pick me up, and we will go out
to the Cathay Inn to celebrate
the beginning of Christmas vacation.
We will order lemon chicken
and egg rolls and fried rice
and those small cups of tea,
and my husband will put my hand
in his, and the baby will play
with his small packets of sugar
and crackers. And after,
we will drive through the snowy streets
to look at the icicle lights
and the old-fashioned fat bulbs
bright as apples in the trees, the kind
my dad hung in our pine the three years
we lived in that house on 19th

before he died. I am too young
not to think of this, or of the boy
with the cold hands
and what it would be like
to wait for him inside his cabin,
to listen to him out there,
chopping and stacking.

FERGUSON'S

It's a diner so we order burgers
and fries, we drink milkshakes
from the milkshake glasses
and they bring the metal
containers they made them in.
Everything tastes good here,
and I stare out at the January sky,
and think of all the times
we've eaten here with your mother
tucked into her coat, drinking
her coffee, waiting for you
to say something.
What will we do next—
go to Rite Aid or Walgreen's?
Buy hard candies for her
to suck on while she looks out
the window and thinks about
how we went to Ferguson's,
stared out across the street
at the shop where her dad used to
cut hair, used to shave her boys'
heads as if hair was a sign
of weakness, hair is what girls have.
This way a man could lift them
by the scruff, like her dad gripped
them, teaching them about pain
and how to stand it,
how to open the door and walk
bare-headed into the cold.

When You Have Lived a Long Time in One Place

things start to vanish. Like the old Newberry's
where I used to buy earrings that looked
like tacks, six pairs for a dollar, and then
go sit at the lunch counter with the old people
eating patty melts and drinking black coffee.
They stared in front of them like the women
on the bus with their plastic rain scarves
that they took from their purses when the bus
lurched towards their stop. They wore dresses
from the old country. Now I wonder
if they have nowhere to go. The building
stands empty like a mind that can't remember
the words that stick things to their places,
pants, chair, toast. How can we remember
if they keep taking things down, like the house
where I lived when I was young and waiting
for love? I lay there in the yard in my bathing suit
pink as a poppy and I could feel his shadow
when it touched my body.
Now there is only a clean slate of grass
where that house stood, the same grass
that covers the spot in Lincoln Park
where there used to be a wading pool
where I took Ben until the day I turned away
to get a toy for him and then he was face down
in the water, and I pulled him out
and we looked at each other and I could see
in his eyes that he couldn't believe the water
was heartless, that it didn't know who he was.

Metaline Falls

The exhibit says Sarah Wise rode her horse 6 ¼ miles to school
every day, wore long underwear under her stockings, and still her legs

sometimes froze. Like the packages of beef in our basement freezer,
all the parts wrapped separately in white paper.

And the zucchini bread labeled with the year so we'd find a loaf
from 1985 years later, coated in ice.

My brothers were so young they don't remember that house or when
I lived there with them. In another picture,

a woman with a white blouse tucked into her long skirt is standing
on her porch, holding a gun.

My friend asks what it would have been like to be the first to settle
    here.
The quiet deepens then, like after tree branches move a little in the
    wind.

Rain hits the windows. And the land without windows
where this woman built a house out of trees and stood in front of it

in the weather, in the arms of the mountains they would mine,
close to the Pend Oreille River.

When my brothers come home, they are strangers.
We bend over our plates, the china from our mother's first marriage

to my father, white with just one gray flower painted in the center,
and I think of her picking them out in a department store

on Long Island in 1967, how she wanted something simple no one
would notice much when they ate

though the evening might feel more important.

Colonel George Wright Shot 800 Horses Here

after Kay O'Rourke's painting, The Indian Wars

I am a fish and a girl and a ghost, hanging
in the sky. Without my clothes,
you can see my bones picked clean.
Beneath me a brown horse buckles
under a brown man. Beneath me blood.
I used to believe the dead were just gone,
but I am not the only skull in this sky.
Remember how you and Annie played
with her plastic horses on her living room
floor and they turned the rug into a field
they ran across, their hard manes flowing?
Annie's house was always dark and her parents
filled it with silence. Annie came over
every morning to walk with me to school
or Swim Team, and sometimes my mom
stepped out of the bathroom and there was
Annie in her thick glasses and chlorinated hair.
In 1858, Colonel George Wright shot
800 horses at Hangman Creek, not far
from here. Every day I drive to work
down Fort George Wright Drive.
Sometimes history is as close as my hair
blowing in my eyes. A horse's muscles
shift under his skin like a kind of light.
Like the way Annie could swim,
lap after lap ahead of me, her body rolling
so perfectly when she did the butterfly
that everyone stopped to watch.

St. Aloysius Gonzaga, Pray for Us

Even though I went to St. Aloysius Grade School
and Gonzaga Prep High School and Gonzaga
University, the only thing I know about you
is that you died at twenty-three so you are a boy forever.
And the story Sr. Geraldine told us:
Once you were playing a game of chess
and someone asked you what you would do
if you knew the world were about to end.
You paused and held your pawn in the air
and then simply made your next move.
I imagined you in a room with a fireplace
like in the films about boarding schools
where the boys all have feverish eyes
and one of them is going to die soon.
Can I call you Aloysius? Was the chess board
marble or wood? Sr. Geraldine was dusted
with chalk and she brought the cold in
from outside. We tried to learn the colors
across from each other on the wheel and sketch
the shadows of fruit but it was difficult
because we'd seen *The Day After* and knew
we could wake up in a world covered in ash
like when Mount St. Helens blew. It wouldn't matter
then that I'd told my mother to buy all those cans
of soup because she would not be standing
where I told her to wait for me outside
the university named for you. No one can be
that calm, Aloysius. You can take my Queen.
But tell me you would have been scared too.
I don't need a saint, I need a sinner.
Let's go back to St. Al's and sit on the swings
in the dark with the kids doing drugs.
Don't you get tired of being the patron saint

of teenagers, all of us followed by fear
like the moon? And the saint of AIDS victims,
the disease I learned about from a pamphlet
my mother left for me on my pillow?
Men were growing impossibly thin like the man
who died of the plague in Rome in the 1500s
whom you are forever carrying.
My mother didn't want to talk about it.
The way she stopped talking about my dad
who also died young and who was always
too good to be true. Aloysius, you had
a beautiful name with the wind blowing
through it and I'm sorry you died
before anyone touched you but God.

FAULKNER'S EMILY

When my students get to the end of the story
and find out Emily kept Homer Barron's
body in her bed for years, that his bones
were a fragile structure of dust, that on the pillow
next to him the town found an iron gray hair
from her head, they say she is crazy, and this
thrills them. I want to ask them, *Have you never
had a secret so delicious you could not give it up?
What would you not do for loneliness and love?*
But then I too would be crazy. I love it when
Emily buys the poison and refuses to tell the clerk
it's for rats. The town describes her eyes
as being strained, like the eyes of a lighthouse
keeper's. I know what it's like to wait and watch.
The town thinks Emily belongs to them, but she
is Faulkner's. The way the trees in their coats
of frost were mine that day last week when
my friend and I stood at the classroom window
in the late afternoon light and she said, *Look,
it's the cover of your book.* Each branch outlined
in ice. I think this must be what Mrs. Newell meant
when she said that if I just followed Beethoven's
notes and his fortes and pianissimos, I would
fall inside his sensibility, a word whose meaning
I can only ever hold in my mind for a moment.
When Emily lost her father, for three days
she would not let them take the body.
Because that would mean he was dead.
"And the town did not say she was crazy then.
They remembered all the young men her father
had driven away, and they knew that with nothing
left, she would have to cling to that which
had robbed her." The other night at the bar,

a song came on and I said to my friend, *This song
makes me think of my mother vacuuming in the house
on Augusta*. And she said, *I wasn't even alive then,
but that's what I thought of too*. That's what it's like
to know the thin book of someone. The dead man
in my bed, the lines the vacuum left in the rug.

GEMINI

Once my windshield was broken
and my boyfriend pretended he didn't
do it. I ripped the tape from his cassette
and threw it out the window.
It's hard to wind the ribbon back in
on those little wheels and sometimes
the tape is still ruined.

A woman wanders out into the road,
puts up her hands as if to say,
Don't hit me, and I want to pull over
and tell her to get in, we can go
for a drink, but my bottle
of antidepressants says, *Avoid Alcohol.*
I used to like Smith & Wessons,
coffee and cream with the vodka
invisible like everything that burns.
When I drank, I could stare out
the window of the bar at the snow
slanting down and not see each flake
falling, just the blur of it, and not see
that man sitting next to me.

I forgot that my sign was Gemini,
my element mercury, the quicksilver
in the thermometers Esther slides
off the table in *The Bell Jar.*
It was me who was changeable
and dangerous.

I keep driving. The woman is gone.
I want to tell her about the poster
I had in my room back then, a Picasso,

a black and white sketch of a man
bending over a woman, the only color
the shock of flowers
growing out of her head.

BUREAU

When my husband asks me where I put the keys,
I say, they're on my bureau,

and he says, you mean *dresser*
and I say, no, *bureau.*

Your mother must have brought that with her
from New York, he says,

and I say, yes, she carried it with its three top drawers
for her silk panties and slips,

her stockings, the small scent sachets she always used,
embroidered like my grandmother's

handkerchiefs, my grandmother who came once
a year to see my mother and her bureau,

who poached her egg in the early mornings
on the kitchen stove. I didn't know *poach*,

didn't know *pocketbook*, the black bag
she opened at the metal, magnetic clasp

and drew out a gold tube of lipstick,
a romance novel with a picture of a man

with his hand on a woman's breast
like the print of the Rembrandt hanging

over our mantel. But that man looked like
he had asked permission, like he knew

he only had this small circle of light
and he should touch the fabric of her dress

before feeling for what was under it,
the skin that had been sleeping

for years beneath a girl's nightgown,
like the ones I keep folded in my bureau,

and the one I took
from my grandmother's apartment in Queens

after she died. It is still in its plastic—
she must have ordered it from a catalogue

when she could no longer go down into the city
but had to look out at it from a great height

so she was closer to the telephone wires
her voice traveled to my mother

like a thin road, winding and black, the kind
you drive at night, the moon always with you.

Now that she is gone, I unwrap her nightgown.
It is pink and sleeveless

and I wear it standing on our porch
so I can feel the wind.

II

When I Think About What I Know About My Heart

I think it has more than four chambers
with tight ventricle hallways that are hard
to fit through. All the walls are the pink of a bar
where I used to go called Madam's Organ.
You don't have to be subtle when you drink.
Because they're chambers, the beds
are curtained in white, and I am lying alone
in each of them, waiting for someone.
Lights come on in different rooms at different
times, like in a play. One room is just
for my mother. One for the dead,
their pillows sunk in from their heavy heads.
I like to go in there. Everything is one color
like underwater. One chamber is my childhood.
A stuffed camel on the floor. A woman
on the wall standing in front of an apple tree.
I counted the apples. The shadows from the hall
blew in their sorrow. One room is where I keep
all my lost boys. They never grow up.
Or love me enough. You understand
why I can't let them go. And here's the nursery,
crib with a hundred acres of blankets
and woods. I am forever standing outside
the door, trying to let my sons cry it out,
but they never do.

You Are on the Green Level

My husband came downtown every day
that summer of Expo '74. His father
was already dead but mine was still here,

standing below me as I rode the carousel,
my horse glossy with flowers. When we rose,
I thought we would keep rising.

You Are on the Green Level,
the sign in the Parkade reminds us,
color of summer, this one and all the others,

and when I leave, I am suddenly
driving through an old summer again,
new at the wheel and turning the world

in my hands. I am picking Kristen up
after her shift and we are going
to her house to stay up late and smoke

and pretend we're grown. Her dad
will make us pancakes when we're hungry,
standing at the stove in his military uniform

and the women's high-heeled shoes he likes
to wear when he gets home,
and I love him for this, the way you love

a true sentence, the one you finally say.
By now my father is dead.
This is the first summer I love a boy

and I don't know yet that kissing that boy
will be under all the other kisses,
like a negative of a photograph, the kind

we don't have anymore so when my sons
find one in a box they ask *what is this*,
and I hold it up against a lamp.

What the Body Does

Our son plays a German child in *Hansel and Gretel*
and dances with a girl dressed in braids and a pinafore
once in Act 1 and once in Act 2 but when they do the show
twice on a Saturday, sometimes she falls
the third or fourth dance.
Later her mother tells me she has cerebral palsy
but she doesn't want him to know.
Like the girl on our eighth grade cheerleading squad
whose muscles snapped like rubber bands
when she tried to straighten her arms
so I tried to hold them for her.
She had a limp and couldn't do the jumps
so we put her in the back row.
She had blond hair though
and a big house where we spent the night
sitting on our sleeping bags in the basement,
rubbing the plastic threads
of the red and white pompoms together
until they curled. We pretended we didn't see
the girls on the walls, naked women in cheap frames.
He must have cut them out of magazines,
but the way they look now in the blue room
of memory is like paintings, their skin thick and pink.
I see him at the kitchen table
after his daughter has left for school,
dipping his brush in the paint and sliding it
like fingers over their breasts which they hold
in their hands like gifts, and they're perfect, circle
of nipple in circle of flesh. And he likes the clean lines
of their legs, how the muscles lie neatly along the bones.
Later when I no longer knew her
I read about him in the paper. They had a day care
in that house where I slept

under the kitchen and heard him open
the refrigerator at night and felt the light go on
and the pressure of the low arches of his feet
on the linoleum. And of course, he touched them,
the young girls in their flat chests
with their arms they could hold up straight.
He was heavy so when he stepped
the ceiling sank a little and I wondered
if the other girls saw but I thought
they were sleeping, I could hear their soft breaths
like a metronome. His daughter was broken
and the basement the kind with fake wood
paneling and orange carpet with bits of food
caught in the shag and stains from the dogs
and maybe he hoped the girls
would help and he didn't think of us
or maybe he hung them there so we would know
what he wanted.
Now when I think of how it felt
to be young and sleep beneath
the cross of a painted woman,
I know that man was wrong.
But I also know that he loved his daughter.
He came downstairs that night
carrying bowls of chips and plastic cups of punch,
and I could see it, the kindness that flooded him
so when he walked he spilled a little
and he was ashamed like she was
of what the body does.

People Don't Die of It Anymore

We're driving up Carnahan, winding south
towards the Palouse, its fields of wheat

at our periphery like hair.
This is the road where Robert Yates dumped

the bodies on his way home
to his five children, hearing the door

click open in their dreams
so later they'll say they knew.

My dad says the retirement home
we just passed, brick and lit with the cold

sunlight, used to be a sanitarium
for women with tuberculosis

and my son asks, *What's tuberculosis?*
We're on our way back

from Greenbluff, constellation of farms
to the north where you go in the fall

for pumpkins and apples
and I can feel their beauty

in the trunk of the car, the thick fruit
beneath the ambrosia's skins, the seeds

we'll have to scrape out of the pumpkins
with a metal spoon and the strings

that will get under our fingernails
and hurt for days.

St. Thérèse Lisieux died of it.
She was so kind in her biography,

always opening the door
for the gardener. And then she started

coughing blood and I mourned her
in my plaid uniform

and my Peter Pan collar.
People don't die of it anymore, I say,

and we fall quiet for a moment and stare
at the houses on Carnahan,

their fences and dark windows,
their scribbles of smoke.

Pentecost

The week after your father died,
I see you walking home after school
in your Wimpy Kid T-shirt,
and I don't even know you, but I want
to call you over like a kidnapper
and tell you it's only beginning.
Your head will always be a lit match
like the apostles in the stained glass window
when Jesus came back. But he will never
come back. I say this because you know
but still you will dream of it.
You will love books and TV shows
about time travel. Like the blue
police box you can get inside and go
back to the week before last.
Or maybe he will find you
like he does in these first mornings
before you remember.
He'll always be wearing the same shirt
when he comes in to wake you,
like my dad in his olive stripes,
as if he never wore anything else.

Accelerated Learning

At the middle school meeting for parents of children
in Accelerated Learning, I sit at a lunch table across

the cafeteria from him. At first, he is just
part of the scene, like the board listing prices

for soda and chips, or the English teacher addressing us,
famous for tearing up a kid's paper if it isn't

double-spaced. She is talking about the importance
of Latin roots, this new language made from taking apart

what they already know. On the first day of school,
my son recited them to me from the backseat,

wearing his new cool sweatshirt and no longer carrying
a lunchbox, his lunch jammed instead into a plastic

bag like the ones he told me the other kids would have.
Port. Carry. Co com con. With. The man's face

is starting to look like two faces, like that optical
illusion of an old woman and a young woman,

the same line for one's chin and the other's nose.
The teacher tells us, *They're going to struggle.*

They're going to fail. They're twelve. Let's face it—
no one here wants to go back to seventh grade.

And then the man leans over to his wife and I can tell
he is saying he wouldn't mind, and that's when I know.

He is the boy leaning back on his chair in Latin
to make fun of Lisa for her pigtails and calico,

her face, scrubbed and chaste. He wore a letter jacket
with his name scrawled between his shoulder blades.

And I was brave and defended her, but he just kept on,
day after day, until she and I both said nothing,

translating in silence what Caesar was doing to Gaul.
Biblio. Book. Scrib. Write. One day this summer,

a group of boys who go to this school were mean
to my son at the pool. *Aqua. Water. Miso. Hate.*

One of them the boy who woke me up
on the first grade campout, crying, asking me

to go find his dad, but I said no. And took
some strange pleasure in his face scrunched up

like that, the way I used to watch my son's mouth
when he cried and waited for a moment

to comfort him so I could see the feeling
quiver there like something almost solid,

something so sweetly vulnerable,
something you knew you could crush.

BROWN IN THE BROWN BRANCHES

It's September so we go to the fair,
walk through the animal barns where

the baby pigs suck and a donkey stands
perfectly still, enduring our attention.

Two girls walk by us wearing Hooters shirts
and short shorts they've pulled on over

thick nylons, the kind I wore under
my cheerleading skirt.

You are young like they are,
and you try to show me with your eyes

you know this is wrong, their shirts
so tight you can easily see the two O's

in Hooters are the wide eyes of an owl,
like the one we saw this summer,

brown in the brown branches of the tree,
night falling, so we had to stand still

for a long time to divide one darkness
from the other. Once I saw a girl

with breasts like that in a magazine
in my boyfriend's drawer at college.

I could not stop looking at her finger
touching where she wanted to be touched.

For dinner we want Chinese food
so we stand in line behind a girl

as young as you, and when she turns,
I see her stomach swelling.

She's getting napkins, a plastic fork.
She orders noodles and rice

and chicken and egg rolls, as much food
as you will eat, my son who has grown

seven inches this year, who has not noticed
this girl is a girl, her face unlined,

like the paper you carry in your backpack
with your binder and books

so you can draw our mountain and our river,
or apples and the shadows they cast.

Douchebag

Here she is in my line
at Albertsons', the girl with the voice
like a flute and the hair
that is part blond and part brown.
When I put on the sunglasses
I just bought, she tells me to take off
the sticker that says I'm protected
from ultraviolet light.
Without her, I would have walked away
and into the sun, proclaiming my safety.
I can't believe this is the girl who yesterday
called my son a *douchebag*.
I think she probably does not know
what one is, has never seen the bag
or its tube, imagined
the women who used it, some trying
to flush out matter
before it became matter,
others wanting to smell like talc
and bathroom windows open in spring.
Oh how they loved the voices
drifting in when they were under
that sheer curtain of water.
She doesn't know about the closets
where it's kept behind stacks of towels,
the humidifier, the box fan, the Tampax
and behind them
the sanitary napkins and belts.
But under her shirt I can see the straps
that keep her breasts from shifting, speaking,
so I know she knows
something, how red threatens like rain.
This must be what she meant,

cloud of blood, bag of water.
She was saying she wants him to suffer.

Briar Rose

Sometimes you do something you shouldn't.
Like when I told the mother I was sitting
next to at the sixth grade graduation
that I was sad my son was leaving

elementary school, and she patted my leg,
and I said, *No, you don't understand,*
and she held her cupcake midair,
and I said, *It's over.*

She glanced at her small daughter
who still had years of tracing her hand
to make a turkey at Thanksgiving
and her teacher wearing her Grinch slippers

to school on Dr. Seuss's birthday
and those weeks every fall
when the homework was Moon Viewing,
which my husband said we never did anyway,

it was always too late when we remembered.
Still I wanted to, I wish we had drawn
the moon every night so we could see
how it was always a little different,

I told the woman, and by that point,
she was staring at me, but I just kept talking.
Sometimes I think he should just go
already, so college won't be out there

like a storm. Haven't you always hated it
in movies when one character calls out

after another but doesn't follow?
Sometimes we do what the story requires.

Like in the fairy tale—they know
the girl is supposed to prick her finger
on the spinning wheel on her fifteenth birthday,
but they leave her to do it anyway.

I remember the first time my son really saw
the moon, I said, when I could see the woman
thought I was done. He was a baby,
and I was holding him in one arm

while I opened the car door with the other
when suddenly he opened his mouth and made
a sound, the kind of sound that just slips out
when you see something beautiful.

July

The air conditioner is dripping
down the peeling paint, and the bathroom
is full of poisoned bees staring at themselves
in the mirror before they die,
and all I want to do is drive, the radio a river
of summers, everything I've lost
flashing in its current.
The car is blowing cool air over my skin
and my arms are bare and freckled
and they still look like my young arms,
the ones I stared at in the sunlight
on the front steps of my first house,
thinking *These are mine.*
No years in the skin, the years
my friend from college keeps talking about
when I meet her for breakfast.
She orders eggs and then apologizes
because she remembers how much
I don't like them, even though
it's been twenty years since she left
her pink coat in the front closet
and then called from Red Deer to ask me
to send it. I went to the closet
and took the coat off the hanger.
It had fake fur and little suede triangles,
and I folded it and packed it in a box.
My friend sips her coffee. Even back then
she could let a pause fall like a shaft
of light. But when I poured too much
rum in my coke night after night,
she poured some of it back, and through
the thin walls of our house I sometimes
heard her crying. She doesn't finish

her eggs and they sit between us
on the table. Soon we will have to go
back outside, into July.

State Line

On the way out to Hauser Lake, we drive
past two cops holding a shirtless boy

face down in the weeds,
past Curley's, fifty motorcycles and a girl

in shorts and cowboy boots, her legs
wrapped around a boy's waist.

That's where we used to go to drink
because it was legal in Idaho.

We ordered Derailers, pink drinks thick
with alcohol, the way this lake is laced

with fish. We can see them when we swim,
their thin skin and skeletons.

My son pulls them from the water, collects
them in the bucket. The fish don't know

he will throw them back. He is tall now,
his shadow long on the dock. We are as distant

and as close as the night he was born
and I lay in my hospital room without him

and heard a baby screaming and knew it was him.
The floors in that bar were wood

and sawdust and I danced on them in my tight
jeans and boots like I was someone else.

We stared at boys we didn't know until they took us
out to the parking lot to smoke. We wanted

something to happen. I am watching my son
from the house. It is getting dark.

The osprey keep lifting off the lake
with fish in their mouths, and the lightning

is pushing up behind the clouds
so all we can see is the pressure of light,

not the sharp bolt,
the way a person tries to speak but can't.

WICKED

Here I am in the middle of my life or maybe even
closer to the end, safe in a house
with a gabled roof like the kind I used to draw
with two windows over the door like eyes.
The house was green and the door was red
like the first house we lived in when we moved
to this town where I've always stayed.
You can't see it but my room has white wallpaper
with pink poppies and the walls are cold.
I know because I am always pressing
my palms against them. Yesterday,
my friend said that in my poems I'm wicked,
as if my poems are someone different,
scraps of paper that fall out of my pockets
that I hurry to pick up. She said the difference
between us is that I like danger. I the one who never
leaves, who stands on my porch looking out
at each morning growing a little colder,
bracing myself for each small change.
I who foolishly had children, forgetting I guess
that they would leave when the weathervane turned
like in *Mary Poppins*, lifted up by their umbrellas.
I dropped my son at the cemetery so he could wander
with his girlfriend among the graves and the rain
and I just drove away, thankful for the slow
unwinding of the spool between us, the years
of gradually touching him less so that now
I even forget sometimes to kiss him good night
and he has to come back downstairs.
I want to be that girl again in my basement room
putting on green eyeliner in my mirror
and listening to Cat Stevens telling me
it was a wild world and it's hard to get by

just upon a smile, girl. I want to be that kind
of scared. It's good to pretend. But summer
is almost over and I have to stop driving around
singing and thinking I'm young. I have to stand up
in front of a class and try to teach them something.
Like how you should leave someone first.
Or how you might think you are a person
who drew a house and moved inside it
when really you're wicked
and always trying to find a way out.

INVAGINATION

My son tells me he's proud of his biology class
because no one laughed when the teacher said

invagination, the word that explains how a cell
takes in food, and I ask what is the root,

so he looks it up and says *vag* means *to wander.*
Like a vagabond. Like how men used to say

women were *hysterical,* meaning their wombs
had come loose and were wandering around.

And then I am singing *Build a stairway to heaven*
with a prince or a vagabond with Rod Stewart

who sang it at my prom where I wore a black
and pink dress that I designed in my head

while I cleared trays off tables at Taco Time.
For a while, I thought maybe I'd keep working

there instead of going to college, rolling burritos
and laying them down in a bin, tucked close

like sleeping children, that I'd keep dating
my high school boyfriend, watching videos

on the floor of his room. I didn't want to jump
onto trains and rattle from one town to another,

I didn't even want to go to the class where
the British Romantics would embarrass me

with their sincerity, didn't want to carry
my thick burgundy book which held

Wordsworth's abbey and Keats's nightingale
and Shelley's heart refusing to burn

out into the rain where the yellow leaves
stuck to the wet pavement would look suddenly

beautiful. One Romantic poem leads to another
and soon you're wandering the moors

and lying down under the stars, drinking beer
and doing your astronomy homework

and the world is falling into you and now
you have a son who knows the word *invagination*'s

scientific meaning along with its potential
to amuse, the same boy who used to jam

his small foot up under your ribs so you had
to press against it to try to make him understand,

through the wall of your uterus,
that he was hurting you.

BETH AND HER PIANO

If you live where you can hear trains,
something is always coming.
Like this summer with its fires
that haven't started yet.
Then it will be your last fall
in this house, sleeping in your room
with the window I used to stare through
at the yellow leaves our first fall
when you wouldn't sleep
and I rode the exercise bike
and tried to let you cry
but you wouldn't stop so I had to come
get you and press you to me
and around your eyes the blood vessels
had burst so you looked like you'd been
through something. For years,
you couldn't sleep without me.
I had to read you *Heidi* and *Little Women*.
Nothing happens to girls. Just the Alps
and Beth and her piano.
She never wanted to grow up.
I've started the slow erasing.
It's better this way.
Like when I was young and I knew
I couldn't leave, so I just stopped
trying so hard. Got A minuses. Smoked
cloves. I won't be able to stay here
with your room still upstairs like a hole
where there used to be a tooth.
No one told me this about love.
That it can be so loud you can't think
of anything else until it's left town.
When you were born,
they had to cut me open to get you out.

Last Night Ferguson's Caught Fire

In the paper we can see the red booths
turned on their sides, their stuffing
leaking out. The fire spread next door

to the Milk Bottle, which is shaped
like the bottles that clinked
on the porch in the first blue light

of morning, at the end of milkmen,
at the beginning of your life.
I went there once with a boy too sweet

for desire, after the Ferris Wheel
and the Octopus and trying not
to throw up on the grass and trying

to be sweet too, the kind of girl
you want to win a stuffed bear for,
one of the big ones that she'll have trouble

carrying, so you keep handing
the skinny man your dollars and his eyes
glint and you wonder what he's thinking

when he folds them in his pocket,
where he's going when he gets off,
not the Milk Bottle for scoops of vanilla

in small glass bowls. His heart is a book
of matches. In the winter, he'll hang
a ragged coat from his collarbone.

He'll think only of this year, this cup
of coffee, as he sits alone in his red booth.
If he walks along a bridge, he might jump.

The river will feel cold at first but then
like kindness. Last night a boy named Travis
killed himself

like young people sometimes do.
He told people he would do it.
They tried to stop him.

Now he'll have a full page in the yearbook,
his senior picture where he's wearing
his dark blue jeans and sweater vest,

leaned up against the trunk of a tree.
I wonder if he felt the bark
pressed against him

when he had to keep staring into the lens,
his cheeks taut from trying.
I wonder if he thought about the tree,

how could it keep standing there
without speaking,
storing all those years in its core.

CATHEDRAL

My summer quarter students loved that story's
ending when the blind man puts his hands
on the narrator's as he draws a cathedral
to show him what it's like.
When I see Cory at the elevator, this is what
I think of. Here we are in coats and boots
after only seeing each other when
it was 100 degrees and we couldn't believe
we had class. Blindness kept coming up,
not as something real, but as a symbol.
Like in *Oedipus,* which Cory liked
but didn't believe. How could Oedipus not
have seen? I don't think I believed it either,
but then I dated a man addicted to drugs
and checked out books with titles like *Cocaine,*
thinking I could fix him. One night,
I had money in my purse, and when he left,
I didn't, and still I had to lie down
and stare at the light fixture until I saw spots
before I could admit it.
Cory has PTSD and can't sit close to other
students. I know the kind of thing
that sets him off, like when Steve comes in
late and tries to participate even though
he hasn't done the reading and halfway through
takes some pills and walks around the room.
Cory wants to kill him. I liked that class.
Linda brought Michael rhubarb, John's shirt
kept coming open. It was the hottest July
we've had, and the sky was full of smoke
from all the fires. I almost told them.

APOLLO 9

Sometimes at night when you fall asleep before me,
I think of your hips, arthritic, mended
with metal, your bad knees, your legs

my mother once said were as large as redwoods
and which now can barely carry you
into the redwoods where we went last summer

and you leaned your tall body up against one
so we could see that even you
could not compare. I listen to your soft snoring

and think about the ten years you lived before me,
about the bulletin board you made in third grade
for Apollo 9, the articles you cut from the paper,

black-and-white photos of the lunar modules,
all this before the astronauts floated across the moon,
pictures I saw in my history book back when

I was your age and it had already happened,
their feet touching the white surface
only for a moment.

These are the years you knew and I didn't
like the years I might live without you.
I will sit in our house and know you are not

coming home to turn on the television, to make
my tea, to tell me when we turn off the lights
that you know I'll be able to sleep.

In college, I could speak French. I knew it so well
I could understand my professors, I could take notes in it,
line after line. Now I open

my mouth and nothing comes out, but if I hear
it again, I will remember the black grate
of the elevator, *un café, un cassis,* a window open

on Boulevard Raspail, the Métro, a pocket of leaves,
all those years before I knew you,
when I thought I loved somebody else.

Spring and Fall

It has been three weeks since your brother died,
thirty-nine years since my father, and I keep thinking
of Fr. Lantry standing in front of ninth grade English,

reading "Spring and Fall." When he asked, *Margaret,*
are you grieving / Over Goldengrove unleaving?,
I thought I *was* Margaret, I thought, *Yes, the leaves*

have always looked so luminous and sad.
In Fr. Lantry's class, if you used "like" incorrectly,
he pointed his long finger at you and said,

"Gettysburg," and you had to write it out again,
even though you thought saying a character was, like,
sympathetic, was better than saying he was,

because how could anyone know for sure how other
people felt? *Fourscore and seven years ago.*
It's all happening again. That old December.

Grief is a house with a door banging open.
Every room holds a silent piano.
At the Gettysburg Museum, I saw the small uniforms

the dead men wore, their muskets, their rusted spoons
and forks. *The world will little note nor long remember*
what we say here. Fr. Lantry liked elegant sentences

like that. I tried to write the whole thing out beautifully
each time. So many men buried under that soil,
and the rain coming down in spring and fall and the dirt

turning over and still the things from their pockets
falling out. *It is altogether fitting and proper*
that we will bury your brother in December. To what cause

did he give *his last full measure of devotion*? How many times
did I write that? So many that it feels like an old coat
I didn't know I still had. I can still hear Fr. Lantry

coming to the end of the poem, *It is Margaret*
you mourn for. And I am still Margaret. The last time
I saw him, I told him what a good teacher he was.

He asked if I had him before or after he quit drinking,
and of course I had no answer. He said after he stopped,
he learned how to say two things: *I don't know*

and *I'm sorry.* I said, *Ah, as the heart grows older.*
I said, *The brave men who struggled here have consecrated it*
far above our poor power to add or detract.

MARY'S WAKING DREAM

What English teacher doesn't love to tell it?
Sometimes I forget my students are there. Sometimes
a flock of blackbirds flies past the classroom window.

In my version, Mary was looking out the window
in the kitchen, her hands in the sink.
"It proved a wet, ungenial summer," she wrote in 1816.

The rain is sliding down the glass in rivulets.
I thought it looked like slow tears when I watched it
out the windows of our old Buick.

Mary wasn't even in the room when the men came up
with the idea. Who can write the best ghost story?
For days nothing came to Mary. Byron wrote,

"Began my ghost story after tea. Twelve o'clock,
really began to talk ghostly." Did that sound
funny to him? It's October here and I plan to talk

ghostly as much as I can. Like this: Byron said
Shelley ran screaming into the room where he was
writing. They had to give him ether. He had seen

a woman whose nipples were eyes. My favorite piece
of art is Lee Miller's eye that Man Ray affixed
to the top of a metronome. For years I felt that way

about someone. It was hard to do anything.
But everything was music. I've been to Switzerland.
When the train pulled into the station,

the sky in the Alps was pink and the snow
held its glow like a heart. I was with that boy then.
It's been almost 200 years since Frankenstein

and his monster came to Mary in a dream.
Then she hardly slept. She could see how the pieces
of skin didn't quite stick, how the Creature had to drag

his too-big body around, how he stood outside
that family's cottage and learned to read and speak
and finally revealed himself to them, but of course

they were frightened. When one of my students says
she didn't like *Frankenstein*, I am incredulous.
Doesn't she know that in 2011 the astronomer

Donald Olson visited Lake Geneva to find out
the exact time of Mary's "waking dream"?
It happened between 2 and 3 a.m. on the 16th of June,

1816. I can't believe the stars can tell us this.
Mary lost her Feminist mother at birth.
Then she lost four of her five children and then

Percy in the ocean. But one night she woke up
knowing that if we create something, it will always
belong to us. Its small wand will swing back

and forth inside you, ticking, until you want
to break it. If it leaves, you'll have to wander
the icy North until it's found.

THE BIG CHILL

I am keeping a list of all the good things
that will happen when I die,
like not having such small sinus passages
or feet so cold I have to sleep with a hot
water bottle like I live on the prairie
with Laura Ingalls, tapping the trees
for maple syrup and sending Pa to town
for flour and sugar and yards of calico
and those peppermint sticks in the glass jars
at the counter. When I'm dead,
I won't have to worry whether he'll get home
safe in the snow.

And I'll finally be done with this hair,
curly and red, never letting the rest of me
go unnoticed, and all those bottles
lined up on the bathroom shelf to tame it
like in the movie *The Big Chill* when one
of the characters regards her own mousses
and gels and says, *Every morning,
another chance to be pretty.* When someone
is dead, you don't think about their hair.
Like my dad's whose picture I pass
every night when I put my sons to bed.
I forgot how rough it felt until Ben's soft hair
changed to the stuff of sponges.

When I watched *The Big Chill* with my mom,
I kept asking who was married to whom
until she was exasperated, but really
it was confusing, they were all there
for a funeral, and no one could tell anymore
who they loved.

At my funeral, I will be done with all of it.
Like that girl I saw walking down a busy street
one cold day last spring.
She did not seem to notice she was naked,
her breasts fantastic, her pubic hair dark
and sudden as a small animal.
She was holding a book, the kind girls
carried to school with their lunch pails,
the kind with a ribbon to mark your page,
something to hold in your hand because
you liked the shape. She didn't look up,
just kept walking and reading, her cold
fingers turning its pages, the paper
so thin you could see right through it,
the print coming off on her hands.

100-Year-Old Box of Negatives Discovered by Conservators in Antarctica

The mold on the picture makes a lattice design
around the door of the *Aurora*
where scientist Alexander Stevens
stands, amazed that after all these years
adhered to the other negatives,
someone has separated and restored him
so even the mold on his picture
fascinates like the intricate shadows
of leaves around a house, the kind of house
he once lived in, he remembers,
reaching far back before the one hundred years
of ice, before the *Aurora* blew off in the storm,
before they even left on the expedition
to stock the depots for Shackleton.
He has dark hair and a beard,
he's wearing one of those pea coats,
and he looks like a man I could love,
his hands on his hips as if daring me to,
as if it were even possible
because what is a century or a continent?
Didn't he travel from Glasgow
to Antarctica to walk across an Ice Shelf
my feet will never touch?
Couldn't I at least do something,
like look out at the sun setting here
in North America in the late afternoon
on the first day of February, 2015,
a thin pink streak above the snow,
and think of him for a moment
standing there in history,
feeling his way towards the pole?

RUINS

The night is a black book, Dave
a wet shadow. We're drinking like we were

too young to do, in three different bars
because Dave says we have to stay

on the move, and we're talking about how
we used to drive the freeway in the middle

of the night, at the beginning of our lives,
listening to music loud, leaning out windows.

I run my hand over the surface of the table
where someone has glued a page

from the dictionary, and suddenly I want
to read all the words, but the past is sitting

across from me. For nights after,
I don't sleep—you don't sleep if you're floating,

no matter how soft your body feels
in the water. It's still water. I never knew

I could get to the bottom of this.
My hand hurt when I was a child

and we had to fill a white page with squares
of different colors, cover all of it with black,

and then use one blade of our scissors
to carve out a design in the dark wax.

This week we are going to a place called Ruins.
I don't know who else will be there—

my black-haired father taking up a whole booth
in the corner, the daughter I never had

rocking in her chair, her hair long and thick
and caught in the slats. She is humming

so loud the waiter asks her to be quiet.
I tell him to bring her the drink

Dave orders, a drink I've never heard of,
dream drink, dark red. She's wearing

one of the sweaters I left in my drawer
in Paris. Black angora with pearls

at the neck. I never wanted to see my head
coming up out of it again.

Let's get out of here. I know a field
with an empty barn. You can see deer

through the blown-out windows
but inside kids have sprayed the walls

with profanity. And isn't that
what this is like?

ACKNOWLEDGMENTS

I gratefully acknowledge the editors of the following publications where these poems first appeared:

Alaska Quarterly Review: "Thinking of You";
All We Can Hold: Poems of Motherhood: "Wicked";
Blue Earth Review: "Ferguson's";
Clare Literary Journal: "Vaccination";
Crab Creek Review: "Invagination";
Enizagam: "Brown in the Brown Branches";
Get Lit! 20th Anniversary Anthology: "Beth and Her Piano";
Hayden's Ferry Review: "The Sunshine Family";
Kahini: "Alaska";
Lilac City Fairy Tales, Vol. 1: "Briar Rose";
New Madrid: "Gloves" and "State Line";
New Ohio Review: "Accelerated Learning" and "Last Night Ferguson's Caught Fire";
Pleiades: "Ghost Clothes";
Poet Lore: "You Are on the Green Level";
Rattle: "What the Body Does";
Rock & Sling: "Cathedral";
Silk Road Review: "Pentecost";
Sow's Ear Review: "Renaissance Body";
Spokane Shorties: "Metaline Falls";
WA129 Anthology: "Colonel George Wright Shot 800 Horses Here";
Willow Springs: "Bureau," "People Don't Die of It Anymore," and "When You Have Lived a Long Time in One Place."

I am also very grateful to all the people at BOA, especially Peter Conners, Ron Martin-Dent, Kelly Hatton, and Sandy Knight. And to my friends who offered thoughtful feedback on the book as it developed: Ann Ciasullo, Beth Cooley, Tim Greenup, Ellie Kozlowski, Kate Lebo, Rachel Mehl, Kathryn Nuernberger, Connie Wasem Scott, Kathryn Smith, Torrey Smith, Ellen Welcker, and Maya Jewell Zeller.

ABOUT THE AUTHOR

Laura Read was born in New York but has lived in Spokane, Washington, for most of her life. She holds degrees from Gonzaga University and Eastern Washington University and studied for a year in Paris and a year at American University in Washington, D.C. She teaches English at Spokane Falls Community College. Her chapbook, *The Chewbacca on Hollywood Boulevard Reminds Me of You,* won the 2011 Floating Bridge Chapbook Award, and her first full-length collection, *Instructions for My Mother's Funeral,* won the 2011 AWP/Donald Hall Prize for Poetry and was published in 2012 by the University of Pittsburgh Press.

BOA EDITIONS, LTD. AMERICAN POETS CONTINUUM SERIES

COLOPHON

BOA Editions, Ltd., a not-for-profit publisher of poetry and other literary works, fosters readership and appreciation of contemporary literature. By identifying, cultivating, and publishing both new and established poets and selecting authors of unique literary talent, BOA brings high-quality literature to the public. Support for this effort comes from the sale of its publications, grant funding, and private donations.

❧

The publication of this book is made possible, in part, by the support of the following individuals:

Anonymous
Angela Bonazinga & Catherine Lewis
Gwen & Gary Conners
Gouvernet Arts Fund
Art & Pam Hatton
Sandi Henschel, *in honor of Rachel Astarte and Khader Humied*
Chalonda Roberts James
Jack & Gail Langerak
Joe McElveney
Boo Poulin
Deborah Ronnen & Sherman Levey
Steven O. Russell & Phyllis Rifkin-Russell
Allan & Melanie Ulrich
William Waddell & Linda Rubel
William Waddell & Linda Rubel,
in honor of Simah, Ethan, and Jeehye